The Future Of Mobile Business

First Published in Germany in 2011
by Tobias Berlin

www.tobiasberlin.com

ISBN: 978-1467957540

Copyright, Disclaimer & Legal Notice

INDEX

INDEX

Tobias Berlin

INDEX

Page No

INDEX

Tobias Berlin

INDEX

Page No

Tobias Berlin

Introduction

About Tobias Berlin

Tobias Berlin was born in Germany and became an entrepreneur whilst at Karlsruhe University studying electrical engineering. In the middle of the 90's he found creating and selling websites so much more interesting than the course he was supposed to be studying and eventually had to drop out in order to have time to build the business he decided would become his future. Although still being registered at university for several years, being so busy building his career, he never went back to complete his degree.

He lives in Karlsruhe, Germany with his wife and two children and has been in business for himself since 1995. During the intervening years he has run a consulting and software company and developed solutions for industrial clients and the premium car companies like Porsche, Mercedes-Benz and BMW. In tandem with that for the last few years he and his team have been creating and developing applications for both Android and Apple.

During the years he has been in business he has experienced numerous ups and downs having gone through different partners and had several companies, which employed anything from 2 to 50 staff. He considers himself very lucky to have survived all the trauma in order to be where he is today.

He says the thing he most enjoys is doing joint ventures with great people and taking advantage of the opportunities that come from these contacts.

He finds having his own company with the freedom to make his own decisions and choices gives him more fun than he could ever have imagined.

Chapter 1

The History of Mobile Business

1995 – The Beginning

The Birth Of The Mobile Concept

I think this was the time everybody was looking to get a mobile phone and the first people already had mobile phones and were proud of them and showing them off a little bit, maybe putting them up on table if they were out for lunch and so-on. Mobile phones were getting cheaper, so people could buy them. The price for voice plans was getting lower, so more and more people were buying them. I would say it was the first step to the mobilisation of the masses. Today, almost everybody has a mobile phone, maybe even a second mobile phone and it is all starting again with the Smartphones.

The Introduction Of Windows 95

Windows 95 was actually the first operating system that everybody using a PC could easily work with without learning all the command line interface or all the difficulties they had previously when wanting to use a PC. It was the first time an advanced fully graphical interface was available where you could use a mouse and click on objects and programs etc. While that concept had been used before on the Apple Macintosh, it was not as common on the PC. It was first introduced with Windows 3.1, but for the masses, Windows 95 was the big move.

After that everybody felt they could learn to use a computer and that expanded the PC from being used primarily in business to seeing it as a tool for everyday use. It opened the PC to everybody, as it is today. Windows 95 in the year 1995 was a big milestone for Microsoft as it changed their corporate identity from being a software company to being a company who was enabling everybody to use a PC as easily as we use it today.

Previously Windows was not a product for the masses because it was complicated. Business people got some training in it and we learned to use the PC through that. But nobody was using it at home because they did not know how to apply a command line interface where some cryptic codes had to be entered to get something done.

Windows 95 contained the first really beautiful graphical interface where a mouse was used to click on objects and icons to start an action. This was quite easy to understand and enabled everybody to operate it. Windows 95 became a major step for Microsoft to move from the business sector to the world in general. People also really discovered Windows 95 as Microsoft was doing extensive advertising to create awareness of it and if you were to ask somebody from that time, they may well remember the big Windows 95 product launch which was the start to everybody using Windows-oriented operating systems on their PC. Today, if you are using Windows 7 for example, it is still the same basic product with a few improvements; it is a little bit faster and requires some more hardware but has the same principles behind it.

General Use Of The Internet

In 1995, people were starting to use the Internet but it was not a mass article at that time. Some people already used the Internet for mailing; some of them used the world wide web for researching information and so on, but it was still not a mass product. A number of people at that time had been early users of online services like CompuServe or AOL but most came from universities where the Internet was already in daily use.

It was also then that the first of today's most well-known companies began; it's strange to think that there was no Google at that time. It was then, for example, that the birth of Netscape occurred, a name that is almost unknown today. So it was the start of something totally new, the really great concept you can see today as a user at home, at work, or even mobile on your Smartphone. The speed was much slower then than today and cordless was not even thought of, the internet was still only available with a land telephone line through cables. But nevertheless it was still extremely exciting because of this new possibility of getting information from anywhere in the world.

For the first time ever you could jump to a website and not even think about where the website was hosted. The connection was there whether it was from Europe, the United States, Australia, in fact anywhere it the world. And even though it was slow, it had a major impact on those using it. It accelerated the gettingof information and the way that information was exchanged with email and even with the first version of some direct messaging systems.

2001 – Mobile Technology Accelerates

Launch Of The iPod

Who remembers when the first iPod came out? The first iPod had a big case and was very heavy with a little hard disk in it. When I saw that version for the first time, I could not believe it had such a big, ugly case and was so huge. Using it was not very handy compared to iPods today but it was the first iPod. It was in 2001 and started a revolution in the way we could carry music around with us and eventually developed into the iPhone we use today. Now you can listen to music on your mobile phone and the iPod was the grandfather of all this technology.

And then, year after year, Apple brought a new iPod to the market and every time it had more memory to save more music and got smaller and smaller. I do not think it got cheaper each time and it may have even got a little bit more expensive, but it had all the other good things and really revolutionised the way of hearing music whilst travelling around.

Did you know that by 2010 they had sold more than 297 000 000 units worldwide!

Another eventual feature that made the iPod so successful was that, in addition to easy access to the music and the content, you had a fashionable piece of hardware and a handy tool for storing your music. This all evolved from just an iPod with the ability to upload your own music.

iTunes Stamps Its Authority

So from Apple's view of the world they had the iPod on the market and they sold a few, but it was not immediately a big success as people could only upload their own music. So Apple decided that their next step should be to offer the public access to all music. Apple introduced the iTunes music store and it as always been a success.

But even so, although people were using the iPod the biggest problem was to ensure that there was enough music and content available for customers to download. To increase the selection Apple decided they should negotiate with four or five of the biggest music producers in the world. It took some time for Steve Jobs and his guys at Apple to complete these negotiations. They wanted all that music in the iTunes store but they wanted it at their price. The goal was to make each tune available for just 99 cents.

As you can imagine the negotiations were long and hard but somehow they managed to convince them that this would be a good move. At the start iTunes had only a few thousand songs in it but was still a great success. And look where we are today. It took some years to become the size it is but today iTunes not only has music but also apps and video. It is a huge success.

The iTunes store itself gives everybody the opportunity of easily accessing music, musical content, songs and even videos and putting them into their iPod, iPhone, or iPad. And the ease with which you can transfer it and pay for it has added to its success. Once you enter your credit card information it is just a few clicks and there you have the content on your device. You can listen to it or watch it everywhere you go; on the aeroplane, in the car, on the train. We just take it all for granted today but there have been quite a few steps needed to get there. Although it looks a little revolutionary it has been just a step-by-step development of technology.

The Internet Grows Up

In 2001, the Internet was no longer a baby; it was becoming a teenager. Many more people now had access to the Internet. Not only people in big cities but also people all over the country. They had faster Internet access than in 1995 and paid less for it. More importantly, there were lots of new services, not only the original email and research ability. We now had free email service, millions of web pages we can look for, service over the Internet, none of which had been available before. In 2001, anyone who wanted to access the Internet could do so and could use it as much as they wanted.

At that time, there were also some new technologies coming in such as DSL (digital subscriber line) which enabled downloading to be much, much faster than before. This opened the way to offer new services like video on demand, where you could watch DVD's being streamed from a web server, movies over the internet or have something like a video conference or telephone conversation over the internet just as people are doing today with Skype. So many new services were coming in, making many more people realise that they also had a use for the internet.

More free services were becoming available such as creating your own web page, so many people started to offer information and services to others by setting up their own web page with information for their friends. More and more content was becoming available on the internet which had not been created or produced by companies but by people for people. And then a few of the first blogging opportunities started. Many other services, which today are really extensive, like Facebook and so on, were started as a single entity at that time.

The iPhone Game Changer

In 2007 we got the iPhone. What is an iPhone? Whilst you can telephone with it, it is not only a telephone. It is a mini-PC, a computing device and it is always connected with the internet. It is like having your home PC in your pocket and always having a connection to the Internet in your pocket. So you get all the information and things you have on your home PC and you can use it on your mobile phone and you can still talk and send short messages and so on and so on and so on.

It is a great device, some people are even today still using the first version from 2007. It was not as smart as today's version and was a bigger, heavier device. If you compare it with the speed and the memory of the latest iPhone it was a fairly basic device but it was the beginning of that new type of smartphone.

After building the iPod and setting up the iTunes service, Apple had almost everything needed to expand to a new area. They cloned the iTunes service and called it the App Store. The same technology and same systems that were already running the iPod were used; that technology plus a few chips for use as a telephone. And they already had some operating systems available because they were building Mac computers, so they just took the operating system and adapted it for the small amount of memory available and for the speed of the smaller device and put it into an iPod to give us the iPhone. They already had almost all the components to set up this new device and so they simply brought it onto the market. As everybody can now see, it was the right time. People readily accepted this forward step and it was a huge overnight success.

A Truly Mobile Internet

One of the coolest things I have seen over the last year is the mobile internet which gives you freedom to receive information almost anywhere you want, as long as there is a mobile signal.

That means you can just take your phone or your laptop or whatever, leave your office, go to a pleasant place like the sea for example and sit there on the green grass working. This is a comfort and a service which would not be available without the wireless internet. As more and more people are going to the internet and more and more technology is fed into it, faster access will become available.

At present access can sometimes be slow. It is okay for typing some text but there may not be enough bandwidth for using some real-time services like getting the full screen image from your office PC transmitted to your laptop. If you want to watch an actual TV show on your mobile device, for example, on a live stream it is not always possible. So it is not yet fast enough for the mobile internet to really work but it will be in a few years' time.

Maybe we should compare it to the birth of the internet itself; now it is wireless internet and things are repeating themselves. As was the case originally with the internet it is expensive and slow but it is getting faster and cheaper every year as more and more people are using it. In the final stage you will have high-speed access with the latest technology. And with the high-speed access the cost for it will go down, so things are repeating themselves.

Just think about what you will have. You will be able to watch videos, watch TV and play multi-player games over the internet with other people anywhere and any time you want. This will be a great way of doing things. It will be a new form of freedom for you. You will be able to work and access the internet wherever you want. It is cool stuff.

The App Store Revolution

The App Store was maybe the smartest move Apple did in all the developing of the Apple iPhone family because almost everything for the App Store was already there. They had very successfully set up the iTunes music store a few years before with an efficient way of billing people for downloading music. They had all the infrastructure for the servers and the data centres where they saved the data all over the world, so they just had to add a few more twists to get more capacity. They added a new logo and adapted the billing and the App Store was up and running. They cleverly used everything they already had and then had a very successful new system to further their already innovative money-making business.

The access to the App Store is still via the iTunes software, which is from the original iTunes store, and sometimes, as a developer, I recognise some structures inside that were always present in the original structure of the iTunes music store. They still work as does the whole system. It makes it possible for people to very easily access new apps and new data with a few clicks including the payment regime. And the ease of accessing the data and paying so simply with total security, no thought needed, makes it one of the most successful business ventures of the age.

No other company has improved on their set-up. To have a central store where everything you want is available, segmented to allow the customer to find what they are looking for in a short time with minimal effort. From an application developer's point of view, another important factor is the payment method. Apple provides the infrastructure to the developer; they make the sale and from every dollar their application earns, they get 30 cents and the developer gets 70 cents. If you think about it, this model has been copied by almost every other company like Nokia with their Ovi Store or Microsoft, they all use the same model and the same percentage. As it has been copied by many other companies it must be the most successful strategy.

Chapter 2
Platforms – The G.A.M.E.

G For Google

Advantages

Now let me explain what is good about the Google Android platform. It is totally free, so everybody who wants to develop for the platform can just download the source code of the development platform, install it and start developing immediately. Because it is free, there is a big community built around it, a big library of books and online courses for you to access and help you to learn very easily how to create your first app. Then because there is no review of your app you can create the app and upload it directly to the store. And so it is immediately available to your future customers.

In this case the process of creating an app is very easy, not very expensive and done very, very quickly because there is no waiting time for a review of the app. With Apple the review takes about 8 to 14 days. When the app is in the review process, Apple looks at it and may decide there is some feature that they do not like and therefore reject it. There is nothing like this on Android. That is a very big advantage for the developer as in a short amount of time you can get many apps into their store. Secondly, you do not have to publish the app in the Google Market if you do not want to. It is actually called the Google Market not an app store so you can go to Amazon and put it in their store or go to another third party app store and put it there. You can even start your own app store such as a

WordPress driven blog with an app store theme and you have your own store running.

So the idea of the open source is still available in different ways and is very easy to start; we will talk later about that concept. However, if you start as a developer, you still have to enrol with them but it is not as expensive as Apple. You pay only $25 to be a registered developer on the Google Marketplace which is a large saving over Apple.

Disadvantages

Because it is so easy to create an app and there is no official checking as with Apple and Microsoft, it is very easy for malicious codes to be introduced by unscrupulous individuals. There may be a free app offering something interesting but hidden in the coding is a virus trying to access some of your data such as your address book or telephone book. There is no review system to check for viruses . The Apple iPhone review would have checked for this and rejected the application without putting it into the market. On Android everybody can create their own app, anybody can set up their own app store or marketplace and the customer has no guarantee against downloading viruses or malware incorporated inside. It allows easy broadcast of malicious apps which anyone can inadvertently download. We have not seen too much of this yet, but I think as more and more people are buying Android-driven smartphones, there will be an increase in its use to get interest from people and encrypt a virus or malicious code which will try to download something or access some data connected to your bill and payment for example. If you are not very careful, you could get a huge bill at the end of the month which is generated in this way. Something like that could happen so easily and is the drawback of this totally open concept and must be guarded against.

A For Apple

Advantages

For the consumer, the user of the iPhone, Apple has a strict review policy protecting their content in their store. Developers always hate this review because they never know if they will get their application through it. It could be that Apple does not like some function incorporated in the app and they will reject it for that. On some occasions we have used icons which looked similar to icons Apple had trademarked or used for their service; they refused that app unless the icons were changed. And there is no discussion, no appeal. The big rule of Apple is their marketer will say, "We like it" or "We do not like it". That is what we developers hate about Apple but we have to live with it.

On the other hand they do check the code for quality and for private API calls, which are not allowed. If an unscrupulous developer is trying to access the iPhones telephone numbers or telephone register this is not allowed and Apple will see this during their review of the app and refuse to put it into the App Store. So, for the customer, it is a kind of quality assurance or service assurance that normally, if you download the app, you can be sure that it should be safe from viruses and of a good quality. Sometimes, when reviewing an app they will even comment on the content saying, "No, this content is too simple or too stupid" and reject it for that reason.

A good example is the farting app. About two years ago a lot of money was originally made with this but Apple have now decided that they have more than 20 farting apps and that is enough. So if today you tried to submit one it would be rejected as an out of date idea, Apple are always looking for something new. Another example is with the erotic apps. We tried at the time to put some in but ours were rejected on the grounds of there being too much erotic content. As it turned out it was not a big problem because shortly afterwards they closed that section. At the time they had about 6000 erotic apps but obviously they decided that they did not want that class of content and threw them out. Some companies made really good money with them. Erotic apps were one of the highest downloaded apps of all time and suddenly, overnight, they lost their business. That is the power of Apple.

It is their App Store and they say what they will and will not have in it, which, most of the time, is a good thing for the customer. However, it is not always the best for the developers but no-one can say that this monitoring is not good.

Disadvantages

So what are the bad points about the iPhone and the Apple platform? As I said before, from the view of the developer it limits what he can offer, but I think from the customer's point of view the idea behind the Apple ecosystem, what I call the Apple Black Box, it sometimes makes it difficult to exchange data from the iPhone to a PC or Macintosh and back. It can be a bit of a closed system.

It is very easy to buy music in the iTunes store, but it is a little more complicated to bring it out of the iPhone back onto your PC or Macintosh. The same thing can be experienced with some data you put in there or even exchange. You have a USB connector and put it into the USB interface on your local PC before you can access all your data from your iPhone. Even then not all of your data may be available; you may need some additional software, for example, just to access all the data. This is something which makes no sense. They have to provide the interface but they do not want to make it too easy for the customer exchange the data.

The same can be said for parts of their Black Box philosophy in the Apple Store, everything is closed. They put everything in the right place for you to encourage you stay inside the store. You do not have to go left or right, it is all already organised for you. But if you do want to go left or right, then life gets complicated. That is just a part of their thinking which is, in my view, the worst part. But everything else is really secure for the customer and as you have one central App Store, not 20 of them, it is really easy for you go there and get exactly what you want with no difficulty at all. Another point is that everything is done well, so that could be said to outweigh the drawback with it.

M For Microsoft

Advantages

Well, today Microsoft is not in the lead and is not as prominent as Google or Apple but I am sure it will not be very long before they are. Each time a new concept arrives in the marketplace they just wait to see if it is the success the launching company hopes it is. When they can see the trend is going to last and they take very little time to join the other developers and offer it. They have enough money and endurance to go there, so they are bound to come up with their own version.

And you can see that they have taken that decision already by making a deal with Nokia. Together with Nokia, which as a hardware provider and is also struggling due to their lack of belief that the smartphone would be such a success so quickly, they will bring out their own smartphone. And I guess, perhaps by the end of this year, when they do launch their new Windows Phone 7 device, we will see that they are still there at the cutting edge of technology. It will take a lot of money for them to make up the ground they have lost and come out with a device on a level with Android and iPhone, but I am sure, in the end, they will do that.

Microsoft are aiming to do something between Google Android and Apple iPhone. They are not totally open like Android, so they have a review process like Apple and also some clear instructions as to what is and what is not allowed in the platform, in the store. But Microsoft would not make money with that so they decided to be even more expensive than Apple. If I remember rightly, they take the same money for the registration which gives you about five uploads of apps free, but after that, it costs you money again. This is the difference. As with Apple they also do a quality check of the code and they do something like a review, but from what I understand, it is not so thorough at the moment because, in order to catch up, they simply have to get more and more apps in their store. So at the moment they are quite open. But later they will be more rigorous. Even so, as they definitely do some quality checking of the code, putting anything with a virus into the store would, I guess, be more difficult than on the Android platform.

Disadvantages

Well, actually the Microsoft store at the moment is not very extensive. They do not have as many apps in there as the Apple iPhone or Google Android Market. Some of the other features they are very good at, such as bringing Windows Phone 7 operating system to more platforms. They made a big deal with Nokia to bring it onto their platform. HTC is another hardware device that uses the corporation. So they are doing quite a good job considering that they joined the race late in the game. But they are just a few leaps behind iPhone and Android, and they will really have to push themselves to come onto the same level with them. From the view of the customer, at present, this is definitely a disadvantage as if you decide to go for a Microsoft Windows Phone 7-driven phone, you will not have as large a number of apps available as you would with the Android system or the Apple iPhone.

E For Everyone Else

So we do have a few more over and above the big three. We have webOS, which was originally from webOS the company. It was developed by some of the guys who were involved in the development of the original iPhone system. They went over to webOS and developed their own version. WebOS already had multi-tasking, a facility that Apple did not have at the time. They had some smooth interface technology which some people thought was an even better clone of the iPhone than the original one but webOS was too small. Last year, it was sold to HP and everybody thought HP would come out with a cool mobile smartphone with a superior operating device. A few days go the newspapers reported that HP will close down the mobile section, it was just not strong enough to play against the larger companies.

Then we have Symbian, which is already in millions of phones, most of them Nokia phones. Years ago they had the Nokia communicator, what I would call a smartphone for the time. You can still get it today. It is still Symbian-driven, but Symbian itself, as an operating system, is too old for many features. It is too slow, too complicated and expensive to develop the necessary modern features for it, so even Nokia itself decided to let it slowly go. They decided that they have the deal with Microsoft for the new smartphone platform. They have introduced Windows Phone 7, so no more Symbian.

Again Nokia developed some smartphones with the MeeGo operating system, which is a Linux-driven version and looked really good. It was considered by some people to be a really good decision but Nokia closed it down when the deal was finalised with Microsoft.

There is still the Bada from Samsung Electronics, who now have the Bada 2.0 on the market. It looks really nice but I am not sure if it will not be on the market for long because if there are not enough developers putting their apps onto that system, very soon nobody will buy the smartphones and then that system will die too.

So I think in the next couple of years we will see all these systems go. You will not see them anymore on the smartphone. In the end, we will see the big ones, Apple with iTunes, Google with Android, and Microsoft with Windows Phone 7, 8, 9, whatever they call it then. Samsung itself is also selling Android driven phones so I would be surprised if that will not the last version because we will see many more Samsung smartphones with Android on it rather than Bada and then, someday, they also will decide to close it down.

Chapter 3
The Four Main Profit Pulling Apps Explained

Business Applications

What are business apps? Typically, one element of the business app is to provide a service or functionality with the focus not mainly on make money, for example, an app for inventory scanning. Sometimes an app is free and you have to pay for a function inside the app, which is then called an 'in-app purchase', or you can get the app free and there is some advertising in there, so it is more like a sponsored app. But typically, you pay for a business app. They are not as cheap as a game not typically in the range of 99 cents or so. Most of them are in a higher price bracket between a few dollars to even $99, which is still cheap if you compare it to the usual price of business software.

Business apps assist with a service you want to provide or a task you want to carry out in the office. For example, you may be used to working with SAP, so you get an app and work on an SAP client app doing some remote working. Other apps give you a method for creating or recording something, creating some ideas, mind-mapping documents, sending documents, creating pictures or modifying pictures. And usually good business apps have excellent support, so if you have some problem with them, you can call or even write them an email and ask for and get a knowledgeable person to help you overcome that problem. Good apps should also offer precise and useful documentation with the app. These are all features which cost money to develop and naturally you do not get them free because the developer is looking to recover his costs.   Also, it is not a game, not a fun app, not dev eloped just for entertainment. It is more a productive app which helps you get things done using your smartphone or iPad. So the business app will cost you money.

Game Applications

Game apps are the biggest segment in the Apple's Store. That means thousands of new game apps are coming out every month and there are tens of thousands of game apps in the App Store. Most of them are well constructed games with good graphics and many can played for hours or even days before you get the final outcome. There are some big brands that have 20 to 40 game apps in the App Store, like Electronic Arts for example but the group of small developers creating game apps and hoping to make good money with them is immense. However, many developers, even some of the bigger publishers, have gone from the paid model to the free model. That means you do not pay to download the actual game app, you get it free. The developer makes his money through upgrades within the app for which you have to pay or selling advertising within the app.

Obviously some of the bigger brands will have the power to sell paid apps. They have the reputation and customer base to sell enough downloads of an app to give them a return on the cost of their development. Developers follow a general rule of thumb that every paid app also gives 10 to 15 free apps for people to download. So you can see that you really need to be a big name in the industry to succeed with a paid app. Even they are sometimes driven to give special one day offers where they reduce the cost of a number of downloads for one day by discounting them by 50 percent in order to increase sales and make the profit for which they had budgeted.

So I would say that, as a small developer, if you think about going into app developing, I would start with free apps. We make most of our apps free and then incorporate other paid channels from which we get our revenue. There are several means to do this as you will see from a later chapter.

Fun Applications

A Fun app is neither a business app or a game app but still very successful in the app stores. Some of the first apps have been, for example, the famous farting apps which came into the app store in late 2008 and have proved to give major profit to the developers with a huge number of downloads. Today there are thousands of fun apps. Most of them do not help you with anything like in a business app; they purely give entertainment without having to play a game or anything; they are just what their name suggests, fun.

It may be some cats which you can make purr by doing some interactive petting. Others when you speak into the app change your voice when it repeats the words back to you, or enable you to take a picture and changes the picture colour, style or style of the picture. Some even allow you to create movies on the fly; you can create movies in the style of the 1920's with black and white pictures and bad quality. So there are a wide range of fun apps on endless topics.

It is not always easy to make a successful fun app. Sometimes it is a very simple idea which works and gets numerous downloads. It is not always important the way you make the app but it is very important to have a good idea which people like. What subject will be popular is rather unpredictable and a bit of a hit and miss affair. You can never be sure any particular fun app will be successful. With a game app it is easier to anticipate what people will choose especially if it is well done with good, playable content.

With the fun app there are certain factors and key elements which if you follow will help you to make a successful app. It is necessary to test the market and adjust and adapt the app. If people do not like it, it will not be a success. The subject can be something which nobody thinks about and which you think makes no real sense. If somebody else makes this app and it is a big success you wonder why you did not think of doing it.

Although it is a bit of a lottery whether your app will work, the fun app is also a huge sector of the App Store. Typically, fun apps are free, again it is the 'freebie' model. The customer gets it free and the developer of the app gets the money through advertising contained within the app.

Information Applications

In the information section of the App Store we typically think about ebooks of which there a huge number. It is bizarre. I have seen examples from a developer who published about 50 ebooks all on the same subject in one run and all looking the same. They were all the same story but in a different language. However, there are some developers who have a few hundred ebook apps in the App Store each covering a different topic and giving varied information. They had already produced them as apps before Apple came up with the ibook app and they just adapted them for the store. It took very little time for the App Store to be filled with these ibook apps; many of which are still available as the original app.

You can get information apps about the weather forecast in your country or even in your location as they use GPS to find you and then give you the weather forecast for there. As you can imagine these are very helpful. Other subjects such as leisure activities, research, training are covered, in fact endless information from numerous websites is available in the information app sections.

Just think about when you are travelling by car. Before, if you were driving for a few hours, you had to put a training CD into the CD player to listen and obtain information on a subject in which you were interested. Now you can have an app for this. In some information apps you can even give the publisher some feedback via an in-built function.

They are sometimes offered free by a publisher as an introduction to them when he wants to just get you as a customer. Typically, the books are in the range of a few dollars, most of them are below $10 and many are even below $5. Training apps can be expensive, as training tends to be, but if you compare the price to some training software or courses on a Mac or PC, even though the app may contain the same or similar content, the cost is several times less by getting the app. This is because the price structure itself in the App Store is typically very low, with the lowest segment starting at 99 cents and going up from there in $1 steps.

Because so many apps come out every day and competition is high some developers consider it to be beneficial to reduce their prices and make more sales. But this is not actually true unless the content is of good quality and the marketing is successful. However, from the customer's point of view, this attitude reduces the average price and the price level itself stays really low on the App Store. A major benefit for those who buy the apps.

Chapter 4
Mass Market Stampede

Bill Gates was Right!

When you think about the mass market in combination with the mobile smartphones, then I can always remember when Bill Gates gave the keynote address at the fall Comdex 1990. This speech was entitled 'Information At Your Fingertips'. It was one of his slogans and at that time he was referring to the mouse and improved connection to information sharing systems getting all the information with just a few clicks on your PC. He was absolutely right because today it is even easier when you are sitting at home using your mouse with your PC. That man has such vision!

Now, with the mobile equipment available, you have all that information with you all the time. And just think, if you forget something or you do not know about something you can take your mobile, type the question into a search engine and look up the information.

I think about myself. Every time I forget something, every time I want to know something I know nothing about, I take the iPhone or the Android and enter the subject in the search bar. I go to Google first and if I am not happy with what I find there I will go to Wikipedia and so on. Google and Wikipedia are the two most common places people search. Even if you need information about words you can go to a translation service or if you want to know about a product you can go to a website, put in the name and see the actual product or an image of it. If you hear the name of a plant but do not know what it looks like you can go to

Google Image and just put in the name and see hundreds of images of that plant.

That is what is so powerful especially as you always have it with you with a connection to the internet available The only problem you will experience is if you are in an area where there is no signal from the mobile network. Then you feel like you are in the Stone Age again. If ever the battery of your mobile is dead and you can not use it you wonder how on earth you lived without constant internet access before it was there.

Today information is available to everybody. It is so easy to get that information, so cheap to get it when you have a smartphone and a connection to internet. I think it has gone beyond the vision Bill Gates had at that time, back when he was talking about information at your fingertips, but the general idea was right, we have information available at our fingertips, anytime we choose. To be totally accurate maybe a finger tap, not a fingertip, a tap on the screen of your smartphone.

Joining Man To Machine

In the beginning, a computer needed a housing with in-built cooling and it took so much energy to calculate a few simple things; it was a monster machine. It took many hours to create a program and many hours to do the calculations and eventually you got the answers and the data. At that time in the 60's and also the 70's, it was impossible to have a computer at home especially as it was so expensive.

Then in the late 70's early 80's came the PC; the personal computer. A computing system which you could have in your house which gave you limited possibilities of working at home on your own private PC. At the time no-one had envisaged where the world wide web would go, how extensive would be our ability to connect to just about anywhere. After that the laptop came onto the market. That meant you could now take your PC with you all the time. It was not stationary at home, you could take it with you and work on it at the café, on the train, on the plane, wherever you wanted.

After the laptop came wireless connection to the internet. So the laptop now operated from this wireless connection enabling you to get data you have saved in a computer somewhere remote from where you are giving even more flexibility. Now, all those opportunities have been brought together with the smartphone. The smartphone is a very personal device. It is not like a PC at home where maybe your wife works on it, your kids play on it and also you work on it. Generally, nobody gives their smartphone to anybody else except maybe for a short telephone call and immediately afterwards you want to have it back.

The iPhone Effect

If you look at the history of information technology or product creation like the telephone or the smartphone, I think there has never been an effect like this. Let us call it the iPhone Effect, where a company such as Apple had not previously been in the business of telephones or mobiles phones. Usually, if a newcomer enters an area of business in which the big companies such as Nokia, Motorola and Sony Ericsson are producing millions of telephones, mobile phones and cell phones every year and appear to have captured that particular market, they will normally fail. Even if they have a new, even revolutionary idea and market it there is less guarantee of success than failure. But if you look at the success of the iPhone, it was just immediate. I cannot think of a similar situation in business where a company, starting from zero sales in a marketing niche, has succeeded in selling up to a few million units every month in such a short time. Apple took the market by a storm.

And then they repeated that success with the iPad. The big companies were trying to sell tablet PCs for many years and were not successful, almost nobody wanted to buy one. Then Apple came along with the iPad, the design was just right and when most of the merchants tried to sell them they sold like hot cakes. Now, all the other manufacturers are jumping on the band wagon and thinking they can sell their PC tablet, but it is a funny thing, it is not happening like that. Some types of iPad clones with Android for example from Samsung or HTC are selling quite well but not the old PC tablets.

It is not only cloning a product that is the answer, the device has to have something special and it seems that Apple knows how to do this. And sure the iPad, with help from the iPhone, was a very smart move in that all the apps run on the iPad immediately. All that together is what I call the Apple effect. It shows that the market is sometimes waiting for the right guy to come along with the right product, market it correctly and it goes like skyrocket. The original version of the iPhone was presented in 2007 and now, after four years, we have the fourth generation of the iPhone and are desperately waiting for the fifth generation of iPhone. Every year there is a new iPhone and every year the technology and the software is getting better and better.

The giants like Nokia are almost out of the business of smartphones, nobody speaks about them. Nokia is still selling millions of featurephones but are not in the smartphone arena. And the other giant, Motorola, sold their mobile phone unit with thousands of patents to a little search engine company called Google and look at the immediate unbelievable changes in an industry in such a short time of 3 or 4 years. That shows the power of the iPhone Effect.

PC Fear Is A Thing Of The Past

I can remember back in the 80's when we kids were playing with our Commodore 64, our Sinclair or whatever device at that time. Our parents had no idea at all what we were doing. And then you would often read in the newspaper and magazines that with the PC coming into businesses jobs will be lost, the structure of society will be killed and everybody will have to learn to use a PC. At that time many people were afraid of effects the PC would have on their work and every day life.

The PC had no good image; it was the bad guy. Thinking about that now attitudes have changed considerably. Our generation and those younger than us are using everything all the time, the PC, the laptop, the Macintosh and the smartphone. We have no fear of them. We are playing, we are using them for daily work, using all of them as tools, as devises to help us in everything we do. We are using them to do research and train, using them as they should be used. This is a big shift from 30 years ago. People were afraid to use the PC and today it is like driving a car; everybody is doing it without a second thought and in many different ways.

Now, especially the smartphone with all the functions it can perform, you can take it with you on your daily journey and take it out of your pocket every time you need it. Check for some information or research, quite a big transformation from the perception of the villain to the saviour, to the good guy.

The Move From 'Feature Phone' To 'Smartphone'

This evolution took place very quickly and when it changed from the featurephone, from a simple phone where you could just phone or send a message (known as SMS) or do some other simple like taking a photo; it gathered immense speed almost overnight. The smartphone, which is fully a PC with the SMS, telephone and photo ability included and with internet ability it even allows video and video editing, it picks up GPS and many other functions that you no doubt know about. There are even sensors integrated for gaming effects. So it really has been in a time warp of between, let us say, 5 to 10 years.

The biggest shift has taken place in the last 5 years, so from 2005 or 2006 when the top featurephones were being used, the jump to smartphones has happened in one or two years. And even today, that shift is continuing because every time with each new generation of the smartphone, additional features are being introduced, new hardware available, faster processors, more memory, extra functions; it just never stops.

Now, for example, you can pay for something with your smartphone. Very soon you will have something like an NFC (near field communication) responder integrated into the smartphone which will allow data to be transmitted by just holding it in close proximity to another device.   This is just another example of how fast technology is moving and people will follow it.

And from what you can see on the market with the apps available and the functions the apps are offering, people are using them and finding no problem with them at all. Once they are on a smartphone, they are motivated to learn every new thing, they understand them and use them.

But this often depends on the age of the user. The younger generation is adapting to it very quickly; they are generally totally into it. Meanwhile, as the smartphone is becoming a mass market product, many older people are also beginning to use it. Some of them are very, very proficient with them, but some are still having problems with all the technical operations required to use these apps. They sometimes have difficulty understanding what is going on with the integration of all the different things and so, I think, there is a certain amount of segregation. I would say that if people older than 60 today buy a smartphone, they typically have the motivation to do this and want to learn how to use it more. Other people in that age group decide that they do not want to be involved.

They are happy with a mobile phone that they can use to phone and sometimes not even text. They do not want or consider they have no need for a smartphone. Some do not even have a mobile phone at all. There will always be this differential, but for the young at heart the more features the better, there can never be too many.

Chapter 5
The Massive Impact On Business

Laser Beam Targeting Arrives

It is absolutely amazing how easily you can laser target your possible customers, your prospects, with apps. Previously, you would do some advertising, TV and radio, press or print medium advertising and the information would be sent out in the hopes that someone would listen to it and relate to your subject or product. Now, with apps installed on the smartphone, you have so many cool possibilities to really reach your possible new customers, targeted by almost any category: age, female or male, city, level of education and even interests. So if you are in a business for dog training, for example, you can target people who are interested in dog training, only showing those interested people your products. This has come about because you can find statistics based on every imaginable demographic for the people using the internet and discover so much about them it seems crazy.

That has totally changed the way we do advertising. It can be absolutely laser targeted. This is especially true when you create an app not for making money but for presenting your business, trademark or brand. It is easy to just create a cool app, bring it out in the App Store, give it away and people will love to download it. That is one of the easiest ways I know to contact your possible new customers and if you include some smart ways to interact with them, they will even give you their name and email address. That is the coolest thing you can have. You know those people downloaded your app, therefore they are interested in that subject and the content you have in there, so it is a perfect way to attract new customers. The next time you have some news to mail, you can contact them and offer them maybe, some trial or information product or special offer. That is really amazingly targeted people and prospects and will get new contacts into your customer base.

Magnetic Client Relationships

So with the help of an app, it is much easier today to establish a good relationship with your customers. Even your prospective customers are more accessible for that first important contact with them and have every chance of their becoming a customer. There are many CRM, customer relationship management, software packages on the market for furthering you relationship with your customers using various channels such as telephone and email and many other methods. However, I think the most direct way is using an app and bringing that relationship into that app.

Imagine an app which directly shows information, news about your business and products, special prices or offers and incorporates your customer contact within it. You can create it so that even if the app is not activated, it will send a pop-up message on top of everything on the screen and give your customer the choice of opening the app to get your message then or later.

If they choose to look at it later they just go into the app and open it in the same way as they would open an email. You can also redirect them via the message to go to another webpage or service or ask them for some feed back on what extra features they would like to have in a product. The possibilities are endless.

There has been some research into the opening rate of such messages and it is tremendous compared to everything else. It is somewhere between 50 to 70 percent which means that percentage of your prospective or actual customers get the message and open it to see the information. It is proving to be a very smart way to grow your relationship with your customer.

Some of these ideas have not been tested yet and technology is moving so fast that there are, and will in the future be plenty of opportunities to set up new ways to relate with the customers and new ways to get them. I am sure that in the not too distant future many more processes will be available for keeping in touch with your customer base.

Think of the many times you have heard people complain that when they wanted to contact a large corporate company, they visited their website and got a telephone number to call. They made the call and where did they end up? They ended up in some call centre and got the impression that their feedback did not have the least hope of getting to the notice of the person they had intended. So they send an email and instead of getting a professional response they got an answer of comment which in no way related to the subject or point they were making. Sometimes they have not received any response at all.

With an app, if it is done well, there is immediate feedback and the feeling that something is happening. Your customer feels cherished and cared for. Even if it is only a feeling, if the message is composed well in a certain way the reassurance is there that someone is listening. So that is a big chance for any business lodge itself directly into the brain of the customer and connect with them, a major change from everything before.

From Passive Advertising To Direct Contact

When advertising is placed in the conventional media, magazines, newspaper, radio, TV it is in a kind of passive way. You have to hope that the person who reads or listens to it will be interested in what you have to say, decide to contact you or even just remember your name next time they go to the shop. Hopefully they will look for you and your product or on not finding it ask the shop owner if they stock it.

That situation has dramatically changed with apps and even the smartphone itself. Imagine the customer may hear about your product from someone else or through your advertising on social media broadcasts and they search for you using search engines such as Google or in the App Store. The next step would be to download the app and get your information directly.

Now you can set up a direct connection with your prospective customer in this new, very smart way. You can very easily maintain that contact with them again through the app and offer additional services. This is a much more active means of advertising and connecting with the customer, not just a passive speculative way as before and gives you an interactive way for you to communicate with them and they with you.

Not only does this make your advertising more active it will also be completely targeted as you can select a certain segment of the market. You can decide if the product is for say the entertainment or sports market and select place it where it will come to the attention of the niche which is most suited to your business. The right people can see it, tap on the advert and get more information.

You can also build social media functions into the app and get recommendations from your Facebook contacts for example, even if they are talking about a product which is not yours. They can inter-relate with your customers and bring more interest to your business. Your business will have an ever evolving content. This is very valuable and can easily be incorporated into your app.

These reasons are why I call it active. Not passively waiting for somebody to come to you but actively going direct to your specific customer and saying hello. This is a mammoth change and is proving to be a very powerful tool indeed to bring traffic and therefore sales conversions to your business.

Hello QR Codes Goodbye Barcodes

QR codes, in a form very like a barcode, are a really a smart invention and they are free. Encrypted behind the code is information the person who generated it wanted to pass on to anyone reading it. Every time I see a QR code somewhere on a flyer or a shop, for example, I want to know what is behind it, exactly what is encoded there. I use my scanner app 'barcode2web' on my smartphone to decode the QR code.

Typically, you get some information or link to another webpage. That is the main effect, to fire up natural curiosity about it and then actually get somebody new coming to your website at very little cost to you. You will have to pay to put the QR code into the product, but it is not expensive and it is really smart.

When I was in San Diego many people cycle there were some girls with a big QR code on their backs, a really big QR code. People were stopping and scanning the QR code wanting to know what was behind it. It was advertising for a body-building studio, so smart. It worked because of the curiosity it generated in those people.

So the QR code itself is like a 2D data matrix code which looks a bit like the white snow on a television after the last movie is over and encoding the information into the system can be automatically done on a PC for example. People have now learned what a QR code is and understand how to scan it with an app and it is a very effective way to connect with them.

You can also track the people coming through your QR code to your website or to your system or even coming through to an app. They will be even more value to your business than your average customers because they are curious and obviously particularly interesting in your business.

The Secret Of Business In Real Time

With a smartphone always connected to the internet and all this power in the hands of the customer, totally new ways have opened up for businesses to interact with them. Let us call this 'business in real time'.

Say you are the owner of a restaurant and you want to offer the customer a discount, maybe 50 percent off a particular meal or something, but you only want this offer to be taken up in the next 30 or 60 minutes. It is now 1 o'clock in the afternoon and your restaurant is not very full and therefore a day when you typically would not make much money.

You still have to pay your employees, your workers, for the premise and all those things. Soon, you will have the ability to make a real time offer such as this to thousands of possible existing and new customers, some of whom will be nearby your restaurant at the time you need them to be. The message will be transmitted into the app and pop up to say, "Hello. Just five minutes from here or 500 metres from here there is a restaurant which is offering food for 50 percent off for the next 60 minutes". Imagine the possibilities this could create.

Another example would be you have your smartphone in your pocket and you are walking in a shopping mall. You are looking for something specific or a particular type of shop and you enter that into your smartphone asking for information. If you have set the smartphone to give you the information you will get up-to-the-minute news of shops in the area you are in and offers that are available.

Both these examples are opportunities for real time interaction between the business owner and possible new customer. Even if you give them 20, 30 or even 50 percent off, you can calculate the benefits to you. If you calculate the cost of your traditional advertising and compare that to the cost of giving them 20 or 30 percent off of your product, in many cases it will be much cheaper using this medium and you get a new customer. The customers are happy; you are happy and you can even get information to be able to contact them again or do a mailing to them. The real time way of connecting and interacting.

Chapter 6
The Powerful Effect On Society

Living, But Easier

With the internet giving total access to all that information we need, life has become a lot easier. The progression through being able to access that information from a PC at home to the ability to access it anywhere on the smartphone has taken very little time but has transformed our lives.

No longer do we have to remember what we needed to know until we got home. We can look that up and get the answer immediately, the hurdles to finding out just what we need are getting lower all the time. We are learning more from having that immediate access and the ability to easily speak to people of authority and knowledge. Not only can we get it immediately, it costs us nothing. It has also revolutionised the way we communicate with both our customers and our friends. Living is most definitely easier with the smartphone.

Payment In The Blink Of An Eye

Mobile payment is a key element in all our lives and has been going on for ages. If you think about the tremendous success of PayPal over the last few years, it is just because it is so comfortable and convenient to use for so many people. I only have to enter my credit card information to access to my bank account once and I do not have to enter it again, so it feels safe. Also I can pay anything from almost everywhere in the world in several different currencies with just a few clicks. It is simple, safe and it goes immediately making it the easiest and most convenient way in the world to transfer money.

Once I wanted to do a money transfer to a country outside Europe. What a painful exercise! I had to go to the bank, fill out some papers and then it took about a week for processing. After one week and lots of commission, the money was transferred. Well, this is something I can do today on the PC at home or at work with a few clicks using PayPal. Imagine all that convenience built into a mobile app so you can pay anywhere you are, at any time. That has actually been developed and is working now and proving to be extremely popular.

This ease of money transfer, again is changing the way we work together, the way we interact and giving much more flexibility and freedom in our lives. You no longer have to stay at home or go home to transfer money. You can do it anywhere you happen to be. I sometimes pay bills when I am on holiday. I can pay an important bill, which I would not normally do on holiday and for which, otherwise I may have had additional late payment charges or missed an early payment reduction.

Society in fast engaging with the efficiency and convenience of payment at the touch of a button hence the increasing attitude of the banking fraternity to withdraw written cheques from our lives.

Instant Global Connection

With the internet and the explosion of social networking sites like Facebook, LinkedIn, and Twitter, it is very easy to connect with people all over the world and that has already changed the way we interact with people we know and find new friends, not only locally or in our own country but globally. We can just so easily find friends with the same interests and the same likes.

The smartphone is giving a new dimension to this also. If you are using Facebook and you have friends from different countries with different time zones, they respond to you, write something on your wall or give you some information at a time when you are not near a PC. They may feel that they never get feedback from you if you can only respond to them whilst on your PC at home or work. If the friend is from Australia and you are from the United States for example, there are so many time zones between you.

Now, with a smartphone, you get the information and can answer immediately, even if you are in bed, travelling on a train or plane you can respond to that contact. Even in business this can sometimes be very helpful. If you get an order or a support question on a Sunday morning, for example and you have a few minutes, why not answer them immediately? When you get into the office on Monday morning how much happier you feel that you have already contacted that customer or answered a few of the support questions. You are ahead of the game.

The Death Of The Office

About 15 years ago I was on holiday in the Canary Islands and we managed to walk up a huge mountain with a beautiful view at the top. I had the idea that I would like to take a picture and send it to a few friends of mine. At that time I had a phone but it was only a basic mobile and could not take pictures or send them; it could not do anything like that. Today, with a few finger taps, it would be done. First, you take the picture, then you generate an email, put the picture in it and send the email to all your friends or even post it on a web page or Twitter and Facebook just with a few taps.

This new technology it is a huge step forward and makes it possible to work and manage life wherever you are, even on the top of a mountain provided you get a mobile network there. No longer do you have to be chained to the office in order to complete that task; it is a great improvement in quality of working and quality of life. Work is nothing like the sweat shop syndrome toiling from 8 am to 5 pm all week; life can be more flexible. You can organise your work round your life. Within reason you can decide where and when you want to do something, when you want to start your iPhone or iPad and look into your things, even if you are on holiday. Everything is not waiting for you when you come back from your holiday, making life much easier and less stressful.

Chapter 7
Endless Business
Opportunities

The New Era Business Promotion

Apps give good new ways to promote your business, your products and your services; given free and filled with content and information about every area in which you are involved. Let us take dog training as an example again. There are many places on the internet where good authoritative information and advice can be obtained free. Create an app with lots of content, some videos, some PDFs, enhancing the training of your dog, publish that in the information segment in the App Store and because it is free, people will download it. If it has quality content and information it will get a high ranking and many more people will be encouraged to download it.

Incorporated within all that information are links to your website or products. You can even dynamically replace that later and exchange it for some direct advertising for your products or services. Once it is installed on the customer's iPhone or smartphone, you can change the content you want to present to them so that the next time it starts up they will see something different. Updating and adapting the advertising will keep their interest and again encourage them to revisit your website. From then on there will be lots of opportunity to interact with them again and again and promote different products and services. An extremely economical and efficient way to promote your business to targeted customers.

Accelerated Brand Building

Several different types of apps can be used to build your brand with the audience you are targeting. You need to get your brand known by as many people in as many areas as you can.

You can use fun apps as a vehicle for promoting your brand information. There have been a few examples in the last year where companies used that very extensively and gained amazing success. The cost for creating that app was a fraction of the normal cost for brand building. Other companies use business apps to set this up but any such app must be of some advantage or value to the customer. It is not enough just to put in some information and hope that your customers download it. They will look at it once and then delete it. You need to think about creating value for them and build it so they will find the app, download and install it and look at it time and time again. Once you have them in this position it is very easy to again update the information about your brand directly into it.

The cool thing about gaming and fun apps is that if they are very good, they will often return to play them again and again, especially if the game is a multi-player or has a highest score element. They will want to continue playing to try to beat the competition and each time they play they will see your message. Your brand will be unconsciously imprinted into their brain. A really powerful way to build your brand.

Multiple Platform Attraction

Today it is essential to use a multi-platform strategy to reach your possible clients or customers in many different ways. This includes on their PC at home and at work, when they log into Facebook, LinkedIn, other web pages and if they visit your web pages. There are many, many different ways you can reach customers and now you also have to include their mobile. This is growing extremely quickly, with more and more people using mobile equipment to visit sites. They are not using their PC but using their mobiles.

So it is becoming increasingly important to use a multi-platform attraction mode to reach customers. If you do not include the mobile and smartphone markets you may be losing 20 to 30 percent of the possible traffic to your website. This traffic will contain prospective customers and you need to attract it to the place where you can give good information and feedback.

Chapter 8
Show Me The Money

Premium Paid Applications

Obviously, today many apps are free, especially in the game section or fun section but it makes sense to have some paid apps in the App Store. For people to be willing to pay your price you need to be either a well-known brand or have an app that is unique or has something special that nobody else has. In Apple's App Store the lowest possible price is 99 cents and the price increases in steps of $1 right up to $999.

Another thing to consider is that a free app, even if it has the same content as a paid app, ranks lower than a paid app, so it is a big advantage to have a paid app. People always feel because they have paid money something is worth more to them. In their thinking, it is worth more so they give it a better ranking. They typically rank paid apps between a half and one star higher in the iTunes ranking, so this gives you a big advantage.

On the other hand, there are some statistics showing a 1:10 or 1:15 ratio of downloads of paid apps to free apps. This means the actual number of downloads of a paid app will not be as high as on a free app so you have to be very careful when considering the price you choose. If it is priced too high, even if it is a good product and something very special, you may not get a very good return on your investment.

It is a good idea to test the market a little bit. Run the app for 24 hours, reduce the price and run it for another 24 hours and see if people react and download it more. If they do, take up the price again. It is a little bit tricky finding the right price. When it comes to business apps they are accepted as being tools so people are willing to pay a price for them but with game or fun apps by a developer whose brand is not well known it is more difficult to persuade them to buy.

Free And Paid Application Success

The free app with an in-app purchase offer has been very successful. That means that you give the app free and get a large number of people downloading it and so get widespread distribution. If they like the app they will tell their friends that it is a cool app and to download it. Inside the app you offer them some more content which has to be bought. Typically this is done for many games apps and other apps which have digital products or digital content, which is generally very easy to sell inside the app.

For example, we once did a fun app called X-doc. It was like an x-ray machine so you could use it as if you had an x-ray scanner. We gave it away with one skeleton inside. If people liked it they could buy additional skeletons of aliens, a sexy woman, an old woman, stuff like that but pay for them. They paid 99 cents for example, to get both the skeleton of the old lady and that of the sexy lady. That is a very successful way of giving the app free to get it widely known, remember the 1:15 ratio between a paid and a free app, and still making some money from it. The only drawback, especially on the Apple ecosystem, is that all the content you put in as an in-app purchase has to go through the

Apple review and Apple also get 30 percent of the money. But that is something you have to live with.

Free Applications With Winning Advertising

Free apps with advertising is one of the smartest models you can go with. As I said earlier, you have the advantages of the free app, people will download it because they love something for nothing. The only thing you have to think about to make money with this model is you have create an app which is what we call 'sticky'. A sticky app is one to which people return time and time again, they have to like the app and then should stay inside for a long time.

It depends on the model, whether it is a business or game app, both of which can incorporate lots of advertising inside. It also depends on the way you get paid for the advertisement and nowadays that is usually based on the number of clicks it gets. Even then there are ways of improving the click rate by the design within the app. For example, If you have a game which requires people push buttons to play, why not put the advertising near the buttons? Sometimes people will accidentally miss the play button and hit the advertising. But I did not tell you that....

It is paramount to create an app that catches people's attention and they like, so they do not just download it and immediately delete it instead of installing and playing it, at least once. Some of the big app advertising providers like AdMob, now actually owned by Google, offer a service to allow you to put new advertising in every 10 seconds.

That lets you very easily calculate your income from them. You get a rough idea of the number of clicks and apply an eCPM, a calculation factor for effective cost per thousand clicks. Typically you get something like between $0.70 to $1.20. Say you get a five impression average in a minute on an advertisement and multiply that by the number people using each app you have and apply the eCPM. You can then calculate your approximate income from that day and multiply it up to the approximate income you can expect that month.

By monitoring the performance of the app and identifying any parameters you should change, you can make small adaptations to get more people in and/or bring them in and get them stay longer. This is one of the easiest ways to make money; give the free app, ensure people like it and that you get a good viral spread and then just get money in from the advertising.

Free Application – High End Upsell

By this I mean a free app which drives traffic on to some other paid app such as a free app which is a light version of the paid app, maybe a free game app. Instead of having maybe 50 levels of the game in the free app, just include 5 or 10 levels of the game which they can play and get interested in. Then you lead them through to a message suggesting they visit the App Store and buy the full version. So the free app leads them onto buying a paid app.

If they like your free app, if it is of a good enough quality, it is likely to get a really good conversion. People will go over to the App Store and buy the paid app, which normally they would not even have known about. With all the free apps out there they would never have even visited the paid apps without having had the opportunity to sample the game for nothing.

You can also use this type of app to drive traffic to a website where you sell products or services or give them detailed information about a product, showing them movies or images and explaining its operation and uses. If they like what you are promoting then you can direct them to the shop on the website. It can also send them directly to the product page where they can order the product immediately with one click.

Yet another way is to create a free app to lead traffic to a site with a CPA offer or somewhere from which you get commission for their entering in data like their name and the ZIP code or postcode where the live. You can put the information into the app itself and then redirect them to another page where on entering the required information you would get paid your commission.

As you can see there are numerous opportunities for you to make money using this type of app.

Chapter 9
Making Your Own
Applications

The Pain Of Learning Programming

For some people maybe the hardest way to create your app is to learn programming to enable you to code them yourself. It can be terribly difficult to create an app, even if you are using the tools Apple or Google give you. If you have gone through this process you will know it takes a lot of time to learn programming. It takes even more time to implement your ideas into developing a system.

So if you really have enough time and enthusiasm to learn programming, why not? There is lots of help out there for you: books, training programmes, software and many other products which you can use to teach yourself programming from beginner to advanced level. So go for it but, before going too far along the teach yourself programming road look into the cost of the information and also the cost of the time it will take you. If you are still sure you want to try, go for it. You could end up as the new star on the programmers' heaven. But if that is not your intent and you see your business going in a different direction, I would recommend that you use someone else's professional service and let them make your app.

Outsourcing – Russian Roulette?

If you do not want to learn programming you can always use outsourcing. It is so easy to go to a website, find a good code builder, explain what you want, pay him or her a few dollars and, hey presto, you have your app. That sounds so easy, but as usual, there can be some surprises in that process.

The first task is to find a good code builder. This is maybe the easiest part because all the sites like Elance and others list the services offered by the outsourcers and rank their ability according to previous customers' comments. So you can see how well the code builder has done on previous jobs and how the customers have ranked the work. That is quite helpful but even then you have to understand the codes and abbreviations used in their success ranking system. But I still think that is the easiest part of the process.

So you find your code builder and you contact him or her and offer the project giving some indication of the budget you are working to. The commission is accepted and a price quoted back to you. The next thing you have to think about is describing what the app should look like, how it should work and what design you are looking for. He is a programmer, a code builder; he is not necessarily a designer. It is very, very unusual to find someone that is a good designer as well as being good at code building. These are two very different tasks.

If you can design it yourself, okay. If you need a designer because, even though you have a good idea, you have not got the ability to design the professional looking app you are looking for, then you will have to outsource this also. You will have to describe the in-built functions you require including that of a user interface, if that is what you want. If you have never done this before you will get an app, sure, but you will not necessarily get the app you want because the programmer may interpret your instructions wrongly and may not get the functionality in quite the correct way you wanted.

So you get the app, whether you are totally happy with it or not, you paid for it and it is submitted to the App Store. Then in the Apple review it is refused. You have to ask your code builder to change it. This could be a few weeks after the time you got the app from them and in between times they have accepted a large commission and cannot work on your app for another six months. So you end up with an app that Apple will not accept and if you are smart enough you even have the source code but you have no code builder.

These are just a few possible problems you should think about before going to outsourcing. Although everybody is telling the same story, that outsourcing is so easy, there are pitfalls into which you can fall and getting out of them can be very difficult and also can be expensive. A fact that is worth remembering when intending to make an app.

The Expert Blueprint

You do not have to worry if you are not good at coding or have never tried to create a code and you do not choose to go the outsourcing route. Today there are some very good sites on the internet where you can put in the required information for the app you want to create and the site itself takes care of the coding for you. This is would not be a high-level, customized app, but is still a good standard and most of them will even allow you to change the colours and look of the app to suit your particular business.

So typically you would have some content from a blog or website, for example with an RSS feed. Take the data from the RSS feed into the app and these app generators create the app around that data. As I say, these are very simple apps but even so can be totally adequate depending on the content. If you have very unique content with images and descriptions put it into a nice app, add a chic splash screen, user-friendly interfacing and your design and let the app creator generate this into your app.

With some of these apps creator sites you can also add images, movies, content from a web page in addition to the RSS feed. Others allow you to set up the look and feel in a more flexible way by adding more tabs and changing the tab names so it looks like it is a totally custom-made app. I would recommend checking out a few of them.

Chapter 10
The Exciting Future Ahead

The Future

Successful business, I have always believed, is built on an appreciation of what tomorrow needs and an anticipation of how to provide it. Thinking ahead and being the first to recognise a need is paramount to eventual success and profits for your business.

The smartphone now is almost an extension of ourselves, almost another arm. People are bringing it into their personal range more and more and it begs the question, "What is coming next?"

Will it be something that is directly connected into our brain? This is futuristic thinking but in view of all the things that have happened in the last few years, who knows what the future will bring. What new idea will change the way we think about ordinary, everyday actions we perform.

I have heard ideas which make me wonder if maybe that might be the eventual step. Not today, not tomorrow but one day. We could easily have a very direct connection to our brain that will recognise a signal to get our awareness automatically. Just think about of that!

Maybe it could be a chip implanted under our skin much like the chip now implanted in dogs to register from where they come, but which has the ability to send a signal to our brain to make us aware of an available product or some knowledge we are thinking we require.

I think about these things all the time trying to envisage what I aught to be developing to keep ahead of my competitors. I am hoping that I can think of an idea before the rest and expand it into the next iPhone or iPad. At present I have no better idea than you what will come next but it is worth thinking about.

What is coming next? What a good question!

Chapter 11
App Generators

App Makr

Anyone who has useful content can use this site to make an iPhone app quickly and easily. It is a browser-based platform which is user-friendly and is comparatively inexpensive when compared to purchasing a custom application. It includes all the desired features of a professional app designed to monetise your content. Setting up an App Makr account allows you to keep track of all your custom-made apps and publicise the promotion of each new app you create. They even offer to handle to whole process of getting your app through the Apple review and bringing it successfully to the Appstore

www.appmakr.com

Apps Geyser

Used by online marketers who are looking for a new channel through which to reach their customers, this site creates Android apps converting existing content into an app in a few simple steps. You really do not need coding ability. And it is free! It is my favourite app maker for creating quick and simple Android apps.

www.Appsgeyser.com

App Builder 360

They offer you a more advanced system for creating your app. They not only accept your RSS feed but they also offer more functionalities like showing images, live feeds, web content, etc.

Even if this is too difficult for you give them the subject and they will build the app, submit it to Apple and you are away. They give lifetime support and have an office-based staff waiting to update or improve your app anytime.

http://www.AppBuilder360.com

Mobile Roadie

Many musicians and bands are using this service to create stunning apps   The site caters for just about any business and can create your app in whatever format and construction you choose. It has three levels of pricing, core, plus and pro, signing up to which will depend on your particular needs and requirements.   They also offer a service which converts any product in just about any medium and incorporate it into an app.

http://www.mobileroadie.com

Mother App

For more that 5 years Mother App has helped leading companies create and publish hundreds of apps for the Apple Store and Android markets. They offer end-to-end app development that helps clients reach their business goals.

http://www. motherapp.com

Introwizard

You need no programming skills as the hands on work is done for you by a team of experts who develop the application and submit it to the App Store for you. Choose your iPhone app from the selection provided and you are on your way to getting an application created free.

All you need to do then is choose your name, add the content you consider would appropriately boost traffic to your website and your App Store details. The rest is automatic and so time cost effective.

http://www.createfreeiphoneapps.com

App Maker Store

A software company dedicated to enabling information to be circulated via mobile phone applications to a company's website. They utilise the latest technology and know how to ensure that you and your customers benefit to the fullest possible extent thus boosting traffic to your website.

http://www.appsmakerstore.com

Chapter 12
Where To Find A Good Developer

It is never easy to find a good developer but there are sites where you can go and hire people with expertise and experience.

These are some of the best sites to find a supplier:

http//:www.odesk.com

http//:www.elance.com

http//:www.guru.com

http//:www.freelancer.com

Either post your project there or contact the developers directly.

Rule of thumb:

Always search for someone who made lots of money through the site (high number of projects and hourly rate) and also have a look at their rating from previous clients.

When you get feedback from them go for the ones who have taken the time to provide you with a very detailed answer and also show real interest in your project.

If you have seen a cool app, why not get in touch with the developer and ask him if he is interested in developing an app for you.

The Future Of Mobile Business

It is always a good idea to a simple NDA.

You can get one here free:

http//:www.elance.com/p/help/supplemental/contract-nda.doc

Some Examples Of My Apps

Business Applications

Inventory Scanner   http://bitly.com/ivs_free

Use this app on your iPhone to scan and manage your inventories. It automates the capture of all these tasks:-

1. Get the product-ID or name of the products via the integrated barcode-reader.

2. Take all corresponding data from every product using the barcode-reader. The app saves that data in its integrated Database for further processing. Add their location, the quantity held, any configurable data you need.

3. Export the collected data by E-Mail or access it from anywhere via the integrated WIFI-Export Server.

Barcode2Desktop   http://bit.ly/b2d_free

Barcode2Desktop is a simple and flexible app to scan and export barcodes in an extensive range of scenarios.

We decode these barcodes: UPC-A|UPC-E|EAN-8|EAN-13|ISBN-10|ISBN-13|Code 39|Code 128|QR Code|125 interleaved.

Barcode2Web   http://bitly.com/barcode2web

* Do you have to enter barcodes into a web **interface**?

* Do you have to do stock taking or inventory tracking?

* Do you want to lookup Product information in a Search-engine?

This app automates these tasks in two simple steps:

1. Use the integrated barcode-reader to read and decode the data from a barcode or QR code.

2. Go to your web page and paste in any the data you need.

Game Applications

City Survivor   http://bitly.com/citysurvivor

Master the everyday madness in the city with City Survivor!

Whether you want to call a taxi, draw attention to yourself, call for help or even if you need a police siren this app will be useful to you. City Survivor does all of these with funny graphics and sounds!

A Hurry Xmas - Antonio and Dodel the heroes of the Christmas season!   http://bit.ly/ahx_free

This is very much a game for the whole family. Everyone can have fun together and even youngest children can join in with the grown-ups having real enjoyment playing it.

Antonio and his brother 'Dodel' are the heroes of this really entertaining Christmas season game. They are set several Xmas challenges, help them to master them.

Antonio's Color Madness   http://bit.ly/aNopoR

Antonio is rewarded for his good work by being promoted to 'Master of Colour' in his factory. Unfortunately he also got a brand-new machine which he has never been taught to operate. He has to discover for himself how to do a very tricky job. Help him solve the problems this task generates.

Soccer2010:   http://bit.ly/soccer2010_free

Become a soccer star with Soccer 2010. Play 4 great soccer games against your friends. These games are in a bundle and you can fight for the highest scores in a global soccer competition.

Fun Applications

X-doc   http://bit.ly/x-doc_free

This is the perfect X-ray fun app. You always wanted to know about the things happening under your boss' suit? You want to know what the lady sitting in front of you is hiding under those clothes? X-Doc brings them all to light!

Glossary

Android – Operating system for mobile phones created by Google

Android Market - Google's distribution system for apps using the Android operating system

API calls - Application programming interface with coding and specification which allow software programmes to communicate

App Store - Apple's official distribution system for its apps

Bada - A mobile phone operating system developed by Samsung Electronics

CRM - Customer relationship marketing

DSL - Digital line subscriber

eCPM - A factor applied to the average number of hits on an advertisement to allow you to calculate expected income from the app incorporating the advertisement

Featurephone - A mobile phone allowing telephoning, messageing and simple actions such as photography etc.

Freebie - A free giveaway used to attract customers and sales of other products

HP - Hewlett Packard

HTC - HTC Corporation, handset manufacturer and network operator

In-app purchase - An offer to buy products incorporated within an app

IPad - A tablet computer used as a platform for audio-visual media developed by Apple

IPhone - A multi-media and internet enabled smartphone developed by Apple

IPod - A portable media player developed by Apple

Live stream - Real time viewing of a remote broadcast

Malware - Intentional virus-bearing code for acquiring sensitive information without permission

MeeGo - A linux based mobile operating system developed by the company of the same name

NDA – Non-disclosure agreement protecting your ideas whilst still getting input from an outside source.

NFC - Near field communication used in wireless technology

Outsourcing - employing someone to carry out a task on your behalf

Ovi Store - The portal for the Nokia-created Ovi internet services

Platform - A framework on which applications can be run

QR code - Much like a barcode but with a higher amount of information stored inside. It needs a scanner to decode and read it

SAP - A German software corporation, the market leader in enterprise application software

Smartphone - A high end mobile phone which combines a personal digital assistant system with mobile phone features

SMS - Short message service

Splash screen - An image that appears whilst a programme or game is starting

Sticky app - An application to which a person will return time and time again

Symbian - The mobile operating system currently used by Nokia

USB - Universal serial bus for connection between computers and electronic devices

WebOS - A linux based mobile operating system developed by Palm but now owned by HP

Windows Phone 7 - A mobile operating system developed by Microsoft

Reference

Join my course '**Mobile Profit Mastery'** to learn how to build a Real Business with mobile apps.

Get the latest news on Facebook.

http//:www.facebook.com/mobileprofitmastery.com

You can join 'Mobile Profit Mastery' here:

http//:www.mobileprofitmastery.com

Hey, if you are on Facebook, jump over and become my Friend:

http://www.facebook.com/TBATFB

Or have a look in my Blog:

http//:www.tobiasberlin.com

www.ingramcontent.com/pod-product-compliance
Lightning Source LLC
Chambersburg PA
CBHW051321170526
45166CB00002B/629